POWERS
AND
PRINCIPALITIES

*"Put on the whole armor of God, so that you may be able to stand
against the wiles of the devil. For our struggle is not against enemies of blood
and flesh, but against the rulers, against the authorities, against the
cosmic powers of this present darkness, against the spiritual forces
of evil in the heavenly places." Ephesians 6:11–12*

Powers and Principalities

inSIGHTS

BIBLE STUDIES FOR GROWING
F A I T H

———

Gene L. Davenport

WIPF & STOCK · Eugene, Oregon

Wipf and Stock Publishers
199 W 8th Ave, Suite 3
Eugene, OR 97401

Powers and Principalities
By Davenport, Gene L.
Copyright©2003 Pilgrim Press
ISBN 13: 978-1-60899-217-1
Publication date 1/19/2010
Previously published by Pilgrim Press, 2003

Contents

Practical Suggestions to the Teacher or Leader

This book is divided into five chapters and each chapter has sub-divisions. This makes it easier to undertake the study for a longer or shorter period of time, depending on the wishes of the group. Some sub-divisions probably will evoke more discussion than others. Below, you will find a list of general suggestions for the overall study, and a list of sources for any who would like to read further on the Powers.

The only suggestion I offer as to discussion techniques is that if your group has more than ten or twelve members, for at least some of the sessions divide into small groups of not less then three and not more than four persons. You will find that some people who will never speak in a group of more than a half-dozen will speak freely in a smaller group.

The following suggestions might be helpful to your group:

1. Assign specific persons in the group the task of bringing newspaper and magazine articles and pictures they connect with the chapter or topic to be discussed in class. Assign different persons each time the group meets. Before asking why the item was chosen, share it with the group or with the small groups and see what connections they make. (Of course, you too may want to select pictures and articles for use.)

2. Keep watch on the television, radio, and movie schedules while the study is underway. Ask the group to watch or listen and to bring to class their own reactions and questions.

3. Ask someone to read something from the *Sources for Further Study* and give a report to be discussed in a meeting of the group.

4. Ask a member of the group to open the meeting with a ten-minute personal response to the chapter or division as a discussion starter.

5. Assign someone to do research and give a brief report on Bible passages to which the author refers that may not be familiar to the class. Then discuss these. Does the group think the author has correctly interpreted the passages or correctly related them to the subject?

Introduction

None of the New Testament writers would have been surprised at twentieth and twenty-first century events most of us view with astonishment and horror. The Holocaust, attempted genocides in Rwanda and central Europe, the use of children as soldiers in Africa and their by clerics in various countries, international acts of terrorism — all these and others the New Testament writers would have seen as terrible, but not surprising, embodiments of the cosmic forces' efforts to destroy God's Creation. They also would have seen as the work of these cosmic forces many things we accept as desirable elements of the modern world. The New Testament writers used several words to speak of the cosmic forces, but the most commonly used English term is *the Powers*.

In this study, we shall consider the origins of the New Testament view of the Powers, the nature and work of the Powers, and the means God has provided to resist the Powers. I shall consistently use the term *the assembly* to refer to the church as the New Testament envisions it. *Assembly* correctly translates the word usually translated *church* in the English versions of the New Testament. I will use *the church* when the subject is the institutional church.

Some parts of the study will require intense concentration. Some parts may evoke anger. I hope all of it will challenge you. The goal is to help you see that the frustrations and confusions that engulf the Church and individual Christians are not the result of mere human ignorance, contrariness, or wickedness, but are deliberate efforts by forces in God's Creation to undermine God's work. Only if we recognize their true nature will we understand how fully we depend upon God for resistance to them.

The Powers That Be

◈

We are not wrestling against flesh and blood, but against the governors, against the authorities – against the universal rulers of this darkened world – against the powers of wickedness in the heavenly realm. Take, therefore, the full range of armor from God, that you may be able to withstand in the day of wickedness, and, having done all, to continue to stand. Ephesians 6:12–13 (Author's translation)

The Complexity Of History. In the New Testament history is a complex drama in which earthly events and heavenly events are intricately interwoven. Human beings are motivated by their own desires and goals, but, at the same time, frequently are the instruments of heavenly forces. We, more likely, assume that either God or human beings are responsible for things that happen. How can an event be the means by which two agents, each with purposes and motives different from the other, work their will?

The Bible has many stories reflecting this complexity. In Genesis 37, Joseph's brothers, impelled by their own motives and purposes, sell him into slavery. This leads to a series of events that culminate in the brothers, their families, their father, and all Egypt being saved from death by famine (Genesis 39–50).

Another example is God's use of Assyria as God's instrument of judgment on Israel (Isaiah 10:5–19). The King of Assyria conquers nations, guided by his own purposes, but also used for God's purposes.

In neither story are the human agents robbed of their own wills, but their actions serve the goals and purposes of God.

The Powers That Be. The Bible does not view history in terms of the actions of God and humankind alone, however, but as also involving participants who are hostile to both God and humankind. The New Testament uses several words to indicate this array of cosmic beings. The English words originally used to translate the Greek terms are *angels, rulers, powers, thrones, lordships, authorities, world rulers, spirits, elements, and elemental beings.* Obviously, our use of most of these words today does not suggest cosmic beings. To us, a *throne* is an official seat for a monarch and *elements* refers to the weather or to parts of a whole. The Greek word *thronoi,* however, refers both to cosmic beings and to monarchs' thrones, and in 1611 the English word *throne* carried the same ambiguity.

A highly influential passage in the English speaking church's terminology about cosmic beings is the King James Version of Romans 13:1–5, with its reference to *the higher powers* and *the powers that be.* This passage, however, has been widely debated. The word translated *powers* (exousia: ex-oo-SEE-ah) has several meanings *(ability, power, those who exercise heavenly power, those who exercise earthly power,* and — by extension — *freedom).* Is Paul exhorting his readers to be subject to the Roman officials or does he also have cosmic forces in mind? Considering Paul's view of the cosmic beings' influence in the world, his words probably have a double meaning. He probably viewed the Roman Empire as one means by which cosmic beings exercise sway over the world.

The portrayal of the Powers in contemporary movies, novels, and some Christian preaching creates difficulty for speaking of them in an accurately biblical way. The controversy over the Harry Potter books, the frequent attack on fantasy literature, the depiction of evil forces in the *Star Wars* movies, and the depiction of demon possession in the recently re-released movie *The Exorcist* imply that the source of evil is subject to spells, enchantments, or sheer human determination. The problem with many of these depictions is their individualistic nature. In *The Exorcist*, for example, the demon possession of a teen-ager results in head- spinning with no ill effects, spewing of odious liquids from the mouth, and the demon's use of the teen-ager to speak in first person. The task then is to exorcise the demon from the girl.

Such a portrayal is rooted more in medieval superstition than in the Bible. The New Testament Gospels' stories of demon possession were to be heard in the context of the entire Creation having come under the influence of demonic forces, under the conditions of what frequently is called *the Old Age*. The individual manifested conditions that afflict the entire Creation. Even the familiar passage about Jesus in the synagogue (Mark 1:21–27) is to be understood on a corporate level. When the demon cries out, "Have you come here to destroy us?" the *us* is to be understood on two levels. On one level, Jesus is overcoming the hosts of demons who hold sway over the Creation. On another level, the us is Judean society. The man is used by the demon to accuse Jesus of works that will bring the Romans against the nation.

The letters of the New Testament portray the Powers as fomenting betrayal of trust, disruption of community, and international warfare.

The threat of the Powers, then, even when their attack is expressed as a problem for some individual, ultimately is corporate.

The Powers As Transcendent Creatures. The Powers are creatures. That is, they are beings God created. In Romans 8:39 Paul, speaking of things not able to separate us from the love of God, closes the list with "nor any other *ktisis* (ke-TIS-is)...", ktisis being something created, built, or developed.

The word *creature* undoubtedly conjures up all sorts of erroneous images. We usually use the word in reference to animate things other than human beings. A creature, however, is any animate being God has created. The Powers, then, are God's creatures. As such, they are essentially good. God did not create anything not good. In the Bible, good and evil usually refer, respectively, to that which is in keeping with God's purposes and that which is counter to or in opposition to God's purposes. It would make no sense to say that God created something out of keeping with God's purposes or against God's will.

The Powers are not ordinary creatures, but are transcendent creatures. That is, their origin is neither in nor subject to time and space. To be transcendent, then, is to be beyond human perception. That God is transcendent, for example, means we cannot see, experience, or meet God directly, face-to-face, but only through God's self-mediation. Similarly, we know the Powers only through their embodiments or through their intermediaries in specific times and specific places. Thus, their existence is not objectively verifiable and cannot be proven to anyone not disposed to believe they exist.

Although all examples risk being misleading, try to imagine something that is invisible, immaterial, beyond anyone's ability to describe, and neither animal, vegetable, nor mineral. Try to imagine it having no beginning, no end, and no age. This may help you see the impossibility of thinking of anything that is transcendent. (Of course, we do imagine things that do not exist, but only by combining elements of things that do exist — such as combining horses and horns into unicorns.)

Because the entire Creation has been corrupted (in theological terms, is fallen), the Powers also are corrupted. That the Creation is fallen does not mean that it is totally evil or beyond the scope of God's redemption, but that its original good condition has been qualified, or compromised, or corrupted. A basic characteristic of this corruption is the universal drives of survival and self-interest.

That the Powers are good means that they still can be of benefit to the world.

That they are fallen means that they can and do cause immeasurable harm. An example of this is the view of the Roman Empire in the New Testament. Romans 13 views the Empire as God's means of preserving order in the chaotic, fallen world. Revelation 13, on the other hand, views the Empire in terms of its demand of allegiance to imperial institutions. In light of the nature and role of the Powers, both views are valid. In a fallen world, who would want to live in a society devoid of secular law and the relative order possible in the Old Age? But who has not witnessed the self-centered, unjust actions of even the most admirable of governments? In a fallen world we need the Powers, even though at times they become demonic.

Some New Testament texts view the Powers as having been conquered and redeemed in the death and resurrection of Jesus, which raises a perplexing theological question. How can the Powers be conquered and redeemed (Ephesians 1:20–23; Colossians 1:15–20) but still so persistently destructive? No answer is completely free of problems, but at least we can say that their having been conquered means that God does not allow them to determine the future. In this world, evil does not have the last word. God can and does turn even the most evil work of the Powers to God's own glory.

When The Powers Appear. The Powers, like God, work through intermediaries. In the Bible, God acts through the actions of angels, human individuals, and various nations. The prophet Amos, seeing the approaching Assyrian forces and calling out, "Prepare to meet your God," was not speaking symbolically. The Assyrians were the transcendent Yahweh's means of judgment upon the Northern Kingdom.

The Bible is not clear on the relationship between the Powers and angels. Sometimes they are listed separately; sometimes their functions overlap. *Malaak* (mah-lah-AHK), usually translated in the Old Testament as *angel*, is defined in Hebrew dictionaries as *messenger*. The New Testament writers translated the term into Greek as angellos (AN-gel-los, messenger), which English Bibles carry over as *angel*. Words from other ancient Near Eastern languages, however, suggest that *malaak* basically means *worker*, or *agent*; and in both Testaments angels perform a variety of duties.

The Apostle Paul, the author of 1 Peter, and the Medieval Church spoke of *angels* and *powers* as separate beings (1 Corinthians 15:24; 1 Peter 3:22). The Medieval Church assumed a rich hierarchy of transcendent beings. On the other hand, Romans 1:1–5 views the transcendent Powers as manifested in the Roman Empire, and in Revelation 12–13 Satan has that role, indicating that Satan is both an angel and a Power. In the final analysis, the unity of the Bible is not a unity of western logic, but is one born of voices in dialogue. The New Testament writers differed from each other in points of view and emphases, and their unity often lies within the tension arising from their differences.

When the angels appear, it may be in spectacular form or as ordinary human beings. In either case, they adapt themselves to time and space. The Powers, too, enter time and space in various guises — through individuals, groups, institutions, ideologies, and a variety of events and occurrences. We experience them as forces and drives that dominate, inspire, and motivate both the institutions of society and the individuals who are a part of society.

The Powers And Individuals. An example of the Powers' use of individuals is the story of Jesus' rebuke of Peter (Mark 8:31–33). After Peter identifies Jesus as the

Messiah, Jesus declares that he (Jesus) must suffer and die. Peter's response is a *rebuke*, a term used to describe exorcism. Jesus' reply to Peter, "Get behind me, Satan," also is a rebuke. The word rebuked indicates that Jesus is not speaking figuratively, but literally. Peter apparently thinks that Jesus has come under the influence of the Powers — that Satan has overpowered Jesus and is pulling him away from his mission. Satan must be exorcised! The Messiah must not die!

Jesus' rebuke indicates that Peter himself has become the instrument of the Powers. They want to persuade Jesus not to continue his mission. If he dies, it means the end of their authority! And who better than the chief of the apostles to persuade Jesus that he need not die?

Questions for Discussion and Reflection

1. How does the description of the interrelationship between God's work and human actions fit with how you have viewed these two? What difficulties do you find in the description in the chapter?

2. How have you heard the expression the *powers that be* used in ordinary conversation? Was it used only in a joking way or was it to some extent used seriously?

3. How do you react to the statement that we cannot know God in and of God's self? What do you think are some places where we know God?

4. Compare the description of angels and the Powers in chapter I with your previous view of these. Does the chapter lead you to rethink your view in any way? If so, in what way? If not, why not?

Old Testament and Ancient Near Eastern Roots of the Powers

The concept of the Powers in the New Testament does not arise suddenly from nowhere. It is a synthesis of several different concepts from the Old Testament, from Judean literature of the second and first centuries B.C., and from ancient Near Eastern literature.

Concept 1: Chaos vs. Order. The conflict between order and chaos was a major concern in the literature of the ancient Near East. The concern was rooted in the perception that human society always is in danger of being overcome by chaos. It was expressed, among other ways, in stories about a battle between a warrior of the gods and a dragon that represented cosmic chaos. From one culture to another, the names of the god and the dragon differed. In the Babylonian version, the version with which the authors of the Pentateuch would have been most familiar, the warrior of the gods, Marduk (MAHR-duke), kills the dragon and uses part of her body to form the heavens and the rest to form the earth. Usually associated with raging, chaotic water, the dragon thereby also was associated with the dominant ancient near Eastern perception of the universe. The universe was widely believed to consist of a chaotic body of water, in the midst of which the earth lay covered by a large dome. Seas, oceans, and rivers on the earth were seen as places where the cosmic Sea emerged, usually in domesticated form. The story of this cosmic battle, though heavily transformed, underlies numerous passages in the Old and the New Testaments. It is echoed in the creation narrative in Genesis 1, in which God brings order into the midst of chaos (the formless, void condition of things at first — Genesis 1:2). God separating the waters is an echo of Marduk cutting the dragon in half. The influence of the story also appears in the parting of the sea at the time of the exodus (Exodus 14) and in the parting of the Jordan River in Joshua 3.

In another version of the battle story, the god kills the dragon by crushing its head. This story lies behind references to the LORD stamping the head of Leviathan (one of the names for the dragon — Isaiah 27:1); other references to the LORD as dragon slayer (Isaiah 51:9; Ezekiel 29:3; Psalms 74:12–14); and the story of the dragon in the Book of Revelation (Revelation 12–13). It may have influenced the story of Jesus walking on the sea (Mark 6:48). In some versions of the story the dragon had seven heads, and in some it was red.

Other examples of the use of the chaos motif are the places where the LORD is enthroned upon the waters and upon the flood (Psalms 29:10), the use of metaphors usually associated with the chaos to describe Jonah's predicament in the stomach of the fish (Jonah 2:3); and the connection, in places such as Psalm 46, between chaos and warfare.

Concept 2: The Gods Of The Nations. The prophets of ancient Israel staunchly opposed the gods of the surrounding nations, gods who often held great attraction for the Israelites. To understand the nature of the opposition and how this later became one element in the concept of the Powers, we must first look at the meaning of the words we translate *god, gods,* and *God.*

The Hebrew word *el* is a singular noun that basically means *mighty one.* The word usually considered the plural form of *el* is *elohim* (eh-lo-HEEM). Several things about these words should be kept in mind.

1) Both the singular and the plural forms of the noun can be used to refer to powerful or authoritative figures both in the heavenly realm and in the earthly realm. Thus, rulers, warriors, gods, and even angels can be called *elohim*.

2) Since Semitic languages do not have different forms for capital and small letters, the spelling of a word doesn't tell us whether to read it as a proper noun (a title or a name) or as a common noun.

3) *Elohim*, though plural, is one of the two words most commonly used in the Old Testament for the God of Israel. Genesis 1:1 can be translated, "In the beginning the Mighty One created the heavens and the earth." Deuteronomy 6:4 can be translated, "Hear, O Israel, Yahweh is our Mighty One, Yahweh alone!"

4) The cultures of the ancient Near East assumed that the heavenly realm was populated with mighty ones able to influence events in the earthly realm. The editors of the present form of the Old Testament believed that although there actually are numerous *elohim* in the heavenly realm, there is only one supreme Mighty One, upon whom all other mighty ones depend for their existence. Although they used the plural *elohim* for this Mighty One, they used *Yahweh* (*the One Who Is*) to speak more specifically of him as the one true Mighty One. In the eyes of the prophets and historians of the Old Testament, Israel often was guilty of attributing to the created mighty ones authority and power correctly attributed to Yahweh, the Mighty One of Israel, alone.

The Old Testament writers dealt with the many heavenly mighty ones not by denying them, but by demoting them. That is, they viewed those that the surrounding nations assumed to be mighty ones worthy of worship (gods) as lesser ranking mighty ones — or angels. That this is the origin of angels in the Bible is suggested by passages in which at least some group of angels are referred to as *children of the elohim* (KJV: *the sons of God* — Genesis 6:1–8) or simply as *elohim* (Psalms 8:5; 82:1, 6–7). It also sheds light on Genesis 1:26, in which God says, "Let us make humankind in our own image." Although later Christian tradition interpreted this as words of the Trinity, it more likely means that humankind was created to take care of the earth on behalf of the Creator and the Creator's heavenly associates — who, of course, were also creatures of the Creator. The mistake of the nations surrounding Israel was not their belief that numerous heavenly mighty ones existed, but their worship of them.

Concept 3: The Angels And The Nations. In some circles of Judean culture, from the late third century onward, the angels were viewed as taking an increasingly greater role in the life of God's Creation. Especially significant was the belief that God had assigned to each nation an overseeing angel. Although this belief seems to have become more prominent in the Greek period of Judean life, it was supported by interpretations of older material such as Deuteronomy 32:17. The Book of the Revelation, toward the end of the first century of the present era, assumed that at least each of the seven churches to which the book was addressed had an attending angel (Revelation 2–3). It is not difficult to see how certain circles of Judean culture might have said, in effect, "Yes, each nation has its own gods (mighty ones), but they are simply the mighty ones (gods) that the Supreme God (The Mighty One) created to serve him."

Concept 4: Satan And His Associates. Prior to the Babylonian Exile, Judean culture gave the heavenly mighty ones (the angels) no specific names or titles. They were simply Yahweh's agents. In the post-exilic period, they began to acquire titles, many of which indicated their relationship to God — or to *El: Gabri-el, Rapha-el, Micha-el,* and others.

One of the mighty ones that received a title that did not contain the name *el* was *ha-shatan* — the Accuser. The Accuser's task, on behalf of Yahweh, was to test human beings to see whether they truly trusted and stood in awe of Yahweh. The Accuser was a sort of heavenly inquisitor. Obviously, this is the mighty one we call Satan. In the Book of Job, Satan is a member of Yahweh's heavenly court. An echo of this task still is heard in Satan's testing Jesus.

Between the time of the Old Testament and that of the New, Satan's reputation became tarnished (to say the least) and several other titles came to be used for him. Among these are *Belial* (the devourer), *the Devil* (the adversary), and *Beelzebul* (the lord of the flies). He came to be viewed as Yahweh's opponent and the Father of Lies.

An important belief in some Judean circles in which Christianity arose was that when God expelled Adam and Eve from the Garden of Eden, God handed over the world to Satan. Thus, the New Testament calls Satan *the ruler of this world*. This belief lies behind the cry "the Kingdom of God is at hand". The word translated *kingdom* refers not to geography, but to dominion and authority, and the proclamation meant that God had now set out to reclaim the world from Satan. Understandably, Satan didn't want to give it up, and the result was warfare.

This stripping away of Satan's authority is the event frequently referred to as Satan's fall from heaven. The Gospel of Luke and the Book of Revelation — the only two New Testament books that refer to this fall — portray it as occurring not before the creation of the world (as portrayed in *Paradise Lost* and by much Fundamentalism), but as a result of God's work in the ministry of Jesus Christ (Luke 10:17–18; Revelation 12:7–12).

Synthesis. By the beginning of the present era, all these elements — Chaos, the dragon of Chaos, the existence of heavenly mighty ones in the service of the Mighty One (angels), the authority of the angels over the nations, the opposition of some of the mighty ones to The Mighty One, and the authority of Satan over the world — had been synthesized into a system in which God was viewed as having turned the entire Creation over to transcendent creatures that sometimes preserve relative order in the world and sometimes bring confusion, destruction, and terror. Even their maintenance of relative order is tinged with self-interest, and when their authority is threatened, they react first by attempting to seduce human beings and then, when seduction fails, with immense violence. This is a general picture of the understanding of the world that underlies the New Testament passages about the Powers.

Questions for Discussion and Reflection:

1. Why do you think society is or is not threatened by chaos today?

2. What is your reaction to the author's interpretation of each of the following:
   Genesis 1:26? Satan? The expulsion of Satan from Heaven? The origin of the belief in angels? The meaning of *the kingdom of God?*

3. Compare the discussion on angels with angels as they are presented in popular articles and books today.

The Powers and Sin

◈

Although there is an intimate relationship between the Powers and sin, the full biblical understanding of sin is obscured today by two developments in western culture — the definition of sin as a deliberate violation of law and the rise of modern science.

The Western View Of Sin. 1) The church in the West was greatly influenced by its absorption into Roman society. Nowhere was this influence more profound than in the definition of sin. Under the influence of Roman culture's pride in Roman law, the church in the western end of the Empire came to understand sin as a willful, deliberate violation of God's law.

2) The rise of the natural and social sciences in the wake of the Enlightenment led to the fragmentation of learning and knowledge. It is now widely assumed that some problems are biological, some psychological, others sociological, still others political, and so on. Consequently, if some issue can be explained in terms of one discipline, the other disciplines are irrelevant. But the disciplines are simply ways of asking questions, and the answers we get depend on the questions we ask. In the matter of sin, some Christians came to assume that if something previously considered a sin could now be understood in terms of the sciences, a theological perspective was irrelevant and could even be destructive of human personality. The appropriate response would not be confession and repentance, but counseling — psychoanalysis, group therapy, conflict management, or the like.

Other Christians rejected the sciences, denying that any understanding other than one gotten from a literal reading of the Bible was relevant. The result has been a truncated understanding of issues by both groups. Many of the reactions to the recent sex scandals in both Roman Catholicism and Protestantism, for example, were either theological condemnations or calls for counseling. From a fuller biblical perspective, however, sin is more complex than a compartmentalized view of the world recognizes, and it is intricately related to the role of the Powers.

A Biblical View Of Sin. In the Old Testament, many words are used to refer to sin, but the three most often used are *chet* (KAIT), *ahvon* (ah-VOHN), and *pesha* (PEH-sha). *Pesha* usually is translated as transgression, rebellion, or revolt. *Ahvon* can mean the act of sin, the guilt sin brings, or the punishment that comes in response to sin. *Chet* refers to a mistake or to having missed a mark, as in missing a target with an arrow.

The significance of *chet* is that it can be used for either intentional or unintentional sin. The concept of unintentional sin is strange to most of us because, as said earlier, our heritage from Roman law leads us to think of sin as a deliberate criminal act. The closest the Old Testament ever comes to specifying an unintentional sin is a reference to unwittingly eating holy things (Leviticus 22:14), but Leviticus 4 in its entirety gives instruction concerning unwitting sin and the appropriate sacrifices to be offered in the wake of such sin.

It may help to understand unwitting sin by considering the realms of the holy and the ordinary. When God created the world, God put things in their own specific places. Some of those things were sanctified, or declared holy (both of which mean set apart as special, as different from all other things). The Sabbath, for example was set apart as completely different from all the other days of the week.

In the Old Testament, then, holiness is not a moral designation, but is a designation of having been set apart from the ordinary. To step over the boundaries between the holy and the ordinary is to violate the order of Creation. This is what lies behind otherwise puzzling instructions such as the prohibition against planting two kinds of seed in one's field or wearing garments made of two kinds of fabric. To mix what God has separated is to bear testimony to Chaos rather than to Creation.

In the Old Testament one can disturb the order of Creation either knowingly or unknowingly, intentionally or unintentionally, but any such disturbance moves the world back toward Chaos, a primary goal of the Powers.

On a more fundamental level, sin is the condition of the entire Creation in the Old Age. Sin is Chaos pushing its way into the ordered Creation. It is not to be understood moralistically, as something a person does, but as a condition into which each person is born. It is a condition shared with the rest of the Creation.

The biblical bases for this understanding of sin are found in Genesis 3, Romans 1, and passages in which Jesus' works of healing manifest God's sovereign rule. In Genesis 3:14–19, the present condition of the world is described in terms of alienation between humankind and the animals, of which humankind was created to be caretakers (3:14–15); excessive pain in childbirth, which was the means of propagating the image of God (3:16a); a struggle for power between men and women, the two facets of the human race, which is the image of God (3:16b); a struggle between humankind and the ground, of which humankind was created to be caretaker (3:17b–18); and the loss by humankind, those who bear the image of God, of the gift of life itself (3:19b).

In Romans 1:24–32, the Apostle Paul describes the present condition of the world as one into which God has handed over the human race. Humankind turned from

God, says Paul, so God let humankind go its own way. The result is a world in which all human relationships are skewed and a Creation that is in agony (Romans 8:22).

Such a view of the world was reflected in those circles that said that God had handed the world over to Satan. When Jesus performs works of healing and exorcism, he is reasserting God's sovereignty over the Creation. This is made explicit by the frequent use of the verb *rebuke*, which — as pointed out earlier — describes exorcism (Mark 4:39; Luke 4:39).

From a biblical perspective, anything that veers from God's original design for the Creation is a sign of the Old Age, a manifestation of *Sin* — not *sin* as an isolated violation of a moral code, but *Sin* as the distortion of the Creation.

The church eventually formalized a list of seven deadly sins: pride, covetousness, lust, envy, gluttony, anger, and sloth. These sins were not actions, but drives that lead to action. They were considered deadly because they were sins committed by means of other sins. Gluttony, for example, is expressed by intemperate eating that disregards others. Sloth, which has come to mean laziness and usually is treated as a moral fault, referred to the emotional distress that comes when one is faced with the harsh realities of life or with the discipline required to live the virtuous life. No one chose — or chooses — to be slothful. Sloth overtakes us and influences our choices. The seven deadly sins are drives that impel us to act in ways that disrupt community, a primary goal of the Powers.

Sin As Corporate. It is crucial that we not understand this level of Sin in individualistic terms. Characteristics of the Old Age are not to be viewed as deliberate impositions on specific individuals because of some act that person or that person's parents have committed (John 9:1–3). Obsessions and compulsions; cerebral palsy and mental retardation; A.I.D.S. and sickle cell anemia; bi-polar dysfunction and various phobias; earthquakes and tornadoes;

homosexuality, gender confusion, impotency, and frigidity; sinus infection, cancer, and the common cold — all, from a biblical standpoint, are symptoms of the shattered condition of the Creation and, collectively, are the work of the Powers. Our various physical, mental, and emotional peculiarities are not necessarily results of specific choices we have made, but are random manifestations of the fractured nature of the Creation under the domination of the Powers.

Although certain manifestations of the condition of the fallen world result in their bearers doing untold evil — such as a Hitler or a Stalin bringing death to millions of people — the proper response of a disciple of Jesus Christ is never, "Well, your share in the fallen nature of the world is more immoral than mine." Comparisons of the morality of others with our own, even if accurate, can lead only to pride. It says much about our scale of values that some churches ask candidates for ordination whether they are homosexual, but do not ask candidates who are military veterans whether as part of their duty they dropped napalm on or in some other way killed children and old people.

Implications Of This View Of Sin. This perspective on sin and the Powers can help to clarify two highly controversial issues in the church today — A.I.D.S. and homosexuality. I select these two topics not because I assume any automatic or necessary connection between the two (which I do not), but because of their prominence in contemporary discourse.

Certain well-known Christian preachers were properly ridiculed when they asserted that A.I.D.S. is the judgment of God upon homosexuality. A.I.D.S. is not confined to any group, but is found both among those who have acted in such a way as to contract it and among innocent victims of the actions of others. The universality of the existence of A.I.D.S., on the other hand, makes it easy for liberals to brush aside any connection between the work of God and

A.I.D.S., except to assure those with A.I.D.S. that God loves them. From a biblical standpoint, both evaluations are incorrect. The existence of A.I.D.S. is a symptom of the corruption of God's Creation.

In an entirely different context, homosexuality is said by many to be a sinful way of life freely chosen and, as such, a primary basis for God's judgment. There is impressive evidence, however, that homosexuality is a genetically based inclination. Consequently, those who think of sin only in terms of a violation of a moral code, can conclude that homosexuality is unrelated to sin or even can encourage homosexual persons to believe that their inclination is a gift from God. There is an understandable tendency here and there to combat dehumanizing social attitudes by claiming that whatever is, is good. Otherwise, it is said, God would not have allowed it to occur or to exist. Such a view is easy to maintain when dealing with that which one favors or supports, but more difficult to maintain when one is dealing with things of which one disapproves. Who, for example, would claim that a genetic inclination to violence is good, because otherwise God would not have given the person that inclination? In a fallen world whatever is, may be necessary (i.e., genetically, environmentally, or technologically determined), but that does not make it any less a symptom of the corruption of God's good Creation, or — in the deeper sense — of Sin.

As for the undoing of individual manifestations of the Creation's distortion and broken condition, we must make a careful distinction between the assertion that those manifestations can be undone by "Christian counseling" and the outside possibility that here or there, now and then, in the life of some individual, God might, for God's own reasons, undo some manifestation or another. The belief that all it takes is individual faith is — because of the fallen condition of the Creation — naïve and potentially devastating for persons who see their own actions as the source of the manifestation.

The Christian assembly has the responsibility to understand A.I.D.S. and homosexuality from a theological
perspective — more specifically, from the perspective of
the Christian gospel. At the same time, because the work
of the Powers can also be described in the categories of a
score of disciplines, the Christian assembly must never
consider the other perspectives irrelevant.

On the other hand, the assembly must never make the
mistake of assuming that since the Powers can be
described in sociological language, they also can be resis-
ted or defeated by sociological methods alone. Legislation
may protect the public at large or groups or individuals
within society, but the preservation of relative order is not
the transformation of the Creation of which the gospel
speaks. It is possible, for example, to pass laws to protect
the rights of minorities, but passing and enforcing laws
cannot end racism. In fact, in some circles, legislation may
heighten racism.

It is ironic that whereas a skewed understanding of the
biblical perspective on sin leads to self-righteousness and
judgmental proclamations, a more comprehensive biblical
perspective, by recognizing that Sin is a condition into
which all persons are born, can provide a basis for a far
more humane approach to the questions, issues, and problems that confront the human race. This does not mean
that the church should ignore the specific manifestations
of the Creation's brokenness, but it does mean that
responding to those manifestations in the light of God's
work to heal the Creation will involve radically different
perspectives, evaluations, and actions on the part of the
Christian assembly.

Questions for Discussion and Reflection:

1. Does the view of Sin as a condition of the world help you or bother you in your view of the world? Give some examples.

2. What is your reaction to the concept of *unwitting sin*? Why?

3. How would you compare the author's description of Sin as a condition with comedian Flip Wilson's Geraldine line "The Devil made me do it"?

4. Are there ways in which you think society or individuals step over the line in terms of God's Creation? If so, what are they? If not, why do you think not?

5. What is your reaction to the author's comments on A.I.D.S. and homosexuality as symptoms of a Creation distorted from God's original purposes?

The Powers in Their Guises

The Powers are embodied in many guises — institutions, causes, drives, and occurrences. We shall look briefly at five examples.

The Powers And The Institutions Of Government. That the Powers are encountered in governments can be seen in two related passages — Daniel 7 and the Revelation 12–13. The Book of Daniel — though set in the time of the Babylonians and their immediate successors — was written in the mid-second century B.C., when Judah was part of the Greek Empire. In Daniel 7 the major world empires that had dominated the eastern Mediterranean world since the end of the seventh century B.C. are represented by four beasts that arise out of the Sea. Their emergence from the Sea indicates their connection with the Chaos. The beasts are conquered and eventually destroyed, and God's rule is given to the people of the Holy Ones of God — Israel. In brief, the author of Daniel views all human governments as expressions of the Powers.

In the Book of the Revelation 13 a seven-headed beast parallels the fourth beast of Daniel 7. The beast in Revelation is portrayed as a facsimile of a dragon in chapter 12 that is equated with Satan, and that the early readers immediately would have recognized as the ancient Chaos dragon. Thus, the author of the Revelation pulls together — as variations on a theme — Chaos, Satan, and world governments. The Christian assembly encounters the dragon by encountering the Roman Empire. Rome is the instrument of the Powers. The connections among Satan, the Chaos, and the Powers' authority over nations indicate

that from a biblical perspective, all human governments, for good or ill, embody the Powers.

The Powers And Nationalism. The Powers' authority over
the nations enables the Powers to deceive us by offering
their own version of one of the things God establishes for
the well-being of the world — identity as a nation. The
problem for the Christian assembly arises in that God has
established the People of God as themselves being a
nation, whether manifested in Judaism, in the Christian
church, or in both (Genesis 12:1–3; Exodus 19:1–6;
1 Peter 2:9–10). God thus acknowledges and builds on one
of the basic characteristics of humankind as God has created us: our dependence on the human race for our identity.
I have no identity and am not fully human in isolation.
This is a primary implication of the human race being the
image of God. We are created for community, and the Old
and New Testaments tell us that, as the people of God, our
community is also a nation.

The Powers choose this characteristic of humankind as
a point of approach. They promise us identity and security
— and, therefore, survival — in nationhood. They provide
authority to govern us, laws to protect us, institutions to
serve us, and decorative symbols to inspire us. The Powers
urge us to find our identity in secular nationhood, and they
promise security in return for allegiance.

Today, one of the most potent national expressions of
the Powers is the National Security State. Historically,
nations have been organized primarily for domestic purposes. The military has been a means of protection when
the nation was threatened from without or a means of
aggression in the hands of a power or land greedy ruler.
If a nation was attacked, all the institutions of government
and each individual member of the society would be
expected to support the "war effort", but warfare was
essentially the responsibility of the military.

In the late 1940's and the 1950's, some nations saw themselves in danger not from a nation or a group of nations, but from International Communism, which was believed to be behind revolutions, social unrest, and agitation throughout the world. Any nation might fear Communists within, from the ranks of both naturalized and native-born citizens. In such a setting, traditional dependence on the military alone was no longer sufficient. In 1947 the United States Congress created the National Security Council and the Central Intelligence Agency. The CIA was a reorganized Office of Strategic Services, an agency for covert operations during World War II. The NSA was a new agency to advise the President on the integration of domestic, foreign, and military policies. Although different presidents have assigned the National Security Council varying degrees of power, the National Security Act gave the military services legal authority to inject themselves into domestic affairs anytime they deemed it appropriate for national security.

The impact of these two agencies can be seen in the handling of foreign military engagements and domestic security for over half a century. None of the numerous military engagements of the United States since World War II have been under a Constitutional declaration of actual war, but war language has dominated each conflict, justifying, each time, putting the nation on a wartime footing. This has been clearly seen in, among other things, the domestic surveillance of individuals, organizations, and groups. The impact of the blurring of foreign and domestic security also can be seen in the militarizing of most local and state law enforcement agencies in their weapons, their training, their uniforms, and their language.

Under the Powers, national security and national survival become the supreme values to which all citizens are expected to subscribe. Although the logical response to such an analysis is that the citizens' well being depends on national security and survival, the problem is that under the self-interest of the Powers, security and survival as the national goal quickly becomes survival as the ultimate goal, which inevitably leads to the narrowing of citizens' rights and the oppression of the citizenry — both of which are the reverse of true security.

Of special importance for the Christian assembly is the way that religion is called into play for purposes of national security. The state, under the Powers, has a religion of some sort, with either gods, a god, or concepts that play the role ordinarily ascribed to gods. (Marxist philosophy, for example, anticipates the eventual demise of religion, but envisions impersonal, cosmic, economic forces as performing a god-like role, insuring the future.) During the Cold War, the United States Congress considered it important to affirm the national religion and the national god on the national currency and in the pledge of allegiance to the flag. No clarification was given as to the specific god in which the nation trusted or under which it exists — the God of Christians and Jews, the god of the Deists, the gods of Babylon, or some other god or gods. One of the most popular songs in the nation during the period was *I Believe*, a song that affirmed that water causes flowers to grow, that even the darkest night knows a candle, and that new-born babie' cries, the sky, and leaves on trees are sufficient bases for religious *belief.*

The biblical writers would have said that the god of this nation, now and in the mid-twentieth century, was not the Mighty One of Abraham and Sarah, Isaac and Rebecca, Jacob, Rachel, and Leah, and Jesus Christ, but one of the lesser mighty ones, one of the angels, or the Powers. Christians and Jews who truly understand their traditions, are faced with a serious dilemma. The People of God are a nation within the many secular nations among which we find ourselves. We are called to give our allegiance not to the secular nation and its values, goals, symbols, and gods, but to the nation God has established on behalf of all merely geographic nations. It was such a dilemma in the first three centuries of the church's life that produced thousands of Christian martyrs.

The Powers And The Holocaust. The Holocaust was not simply an attempt by a political-military-religious movement to destroy the people of one religion among many. It also was the effort of the Powers to destroy the people God had created to be the means of the world's liberation from the Powers. The Nazi Party was the willing, assenting instrument of the Powers in a technological, bureaucratic program, of which Hitler was the central assenting figure.

This is not to deny that roughly the same number of Jews and non-Jews died in the Holocaust (five to six million mentally retarded persons, persons with physical deformities and chronic diseases, homosexuals, Romani — commonly called Gypsies — and Jehovah's Witnesses also were killed) or that Hitler's stated goal was the so-called purification of the German people. These facts simply exemplify the craftiness of the Powers. Hitler's stated goal of racial purification made it possible later for some to argue against the significance of the attack on the Jews.

The Powers attacked the Jews because the Jews continue as the elect People of God (Romans 9:4–5), the community established as God's instrument of blessing for the world. Israel would be the means by which the consequences of the Fall would be undone. The Powers cannot tolerate such a community. It must be destroyed; but the destruction must be done in such a way that its true nature is veiled. This was the function of Hitler's obsession with the so-called purification of the German people.

It is irrelevant that many of the Jews who died in the Holocaust were not lineal descendents of the patriarchs and matriarchs. All converts and descendents of converts in Judaism have their identity through bonding with the lineal descendents.

The full significance of the Holocaust, however, lies deeper still. In the cross of the Israelite Jesus, God was at work continuing the blessing and liberation of the world. This did not displace Israel from its task, but made it possible for Israel, through unity with the Messiah, to fulfill the task. Moreover, in the cross of the Messiah God also opens a door to the inclusion of Gentiles into Israel. In baptism the Christian assembly is incorporated, as a community, into the death of Jesus, and since Jesus is the Messiah of Israel, baptism binds the assembly to Israel. Through baptism the assembly becomes a participant in God's redeeming work.

The Powers cannot tolerate this. They attempted to undo God's work by the crucifixion of Jesus. Various New Testament writers make clear that the cross was the work of the Powers (Luke 22:3; John 13:2). What the Powers instigated, however, was the means of their defeat. Had they understood this, wrote Paul, "they would not have crucified the Monarch of Glory" (1 Corinthians 2:8).

The crucifixion of Jesus and the Holocaust are the two major events — though not the only events — in which the Powers, represented by Satan, sought to undermine God's redemption by the destruction of the instrument of redemption. Humankind had been created to exercise dominion over the world on God's behalf. That dominion had been handed over to the Powers, and the liberation of humankind would mean loss of dominion for the Powers. Keeping humankind in bondage would be a blow to God's own plan and to God's power and authority.

It seems quite likely that had Hitler been successful in destroying the Jews — at least the Jews of Europe — the next step would have been an overt attack upon Christianity. He already had established the ecclesiastical machinery by means of which many Christians gave full support to the Nazi government. The Christians who gave that support are remembered today as *The German Christians.* Hitler also desired, however, to turn Christian ceremonies into ceremonies of nature rather than events of the Christian gospel and to turn Christian symbols into symbols of nature. By destroying the Jews and either destroying or transforming the church, the Powers presumed they would undo both the Exodus and the Crucifixion and Resurrection, thereby undermining the Creation and condemning the world to Chaos and Death.

The Powers And Language: Freedom and Justice. The Powers corrupt our use of language by seducing us into using innocent and attractive words for self-serving and heinous acts. *Freedom* is a good example. Freedom often is defined as the right to do what you want to do as long as it doesn't interfere with someone else's rights. This definition also is reflected in expressions such as, "One of the great things about the United States is the freedom to worship as we want to." I have sometimes been scolded that men and women died in wars to give me the freedom to believe and preach as I do. Here, too, freedom is being defined as the right to do something I want to do.

The Apostle Paul confronted a similar confusion in the Christian assembly at Corinth. Some there viewed freedom as the elimination of constraints — even ignoring whether someone else was harmed by their actions. Two examples are: 1) the congregation's approval of a form of incest (Corinthians 5:1–2); and 2) the assumption by some that whether to eat meat that had been sacrificed to idols was to be determined by their own freedom, rather than by the effect the act might have on less mature members of the congregation (1 Corinthians 8:4–12). Paul saw these not as expressions of freedom, but as signs of slavery to the self-interest (*sarx*, usually translated *the flesh*) of the Old Age. According to Paul, everyone is a slave — either to sin or to Christ (Romans 6:15–19) — and slavery to

Christ is freedom from self-interest. The Powers convince us that slavery to self-interest is freedom. Consider, for example, the person who breaks out of a marriage because he or she must be "free" to "discover who he or she is." Or consider the congregation that makes its decisions on the basis of survival, rather than on the imitation of Jesus, who died that others might live.

The Powers also seduce us in our language about *justice*. The word usually translated justice in the Old Testament is *mishpat* (MISH-pot), from a verb that means *to set things right* or *to restore equilibrium*. The judges in the Old Testament were military leaders whom God raised up to cast off the yoke of slavery from neighboring peoples, to restore order. *In theory*, this also is what secular courts are established to do. Crime disrupts the social order. The justice system is to restore equilibrium. In reality, the world's legal systems engage not in restoration of equilibrium, but in revenge.

Capital punishment is a classic example. In the Old Testament capital punishment first is prescribed for the preservation of the human race because the human race is in the image of God (Genesis 9:6). Later, it is for the expulsion of evil from Israel, the holy community (Leviticus 20). If Israel becomes a community like the nations, thereby losing its holiness, the blessing of the world will be at stake. Later still, in the New Testament, it is acknowledged that the Roman Emperor — who is under the authority of the Powers and is in charge of affairs of the Old Age — has authority to execute (Romans 13:3–5), but the Christian assembly is prohibited from harming even the enemy. On the contrary, it is called to love the enemy (Matthew 5:38–47).

The Powers persuade us that revenge is justice. When Byron De La Beckwith was convicted, in 1994, for the 1963 murder of Medgar Evers, some newspaper headlines said that justice finally had been done. The biblical definition of justice suggests, however, that justice truly will have been achieved only when Byron De La Beckwith and Medgar Evers embrace before the throne of God — De La Beckwith asking Evers for forgiveness and Evers telling De La Beckwith that he loves him.

The question is not whether people should be protected from murderers (which the Powers do up to a point), whether racial oppression is a sin (all oppression is sin), or whether the judicial system should simply forgive criminals (it should not unless that forgiveness contributes to the relative order of the fallen world). The question is whether what the Powers call justice is justice from God's standpoint. It would seem that the answer is *no.* Jesus said that we are to love our enemies. The Powers tell us that we are to hate our enemies and seek their death.

The Powers And Political Correctness. Recognizing the Powers in things commonly viewed as destructive is, for those who believe the Powers exist, relatively easy. It does not take a great deal of wisdom to recognize their presence in racism, militarism, nationalism, and in persons or groups we don't like. Recognizing them when they invade our own minds and the minds of groups to which we have given our allegiance is not so easy. The Powers find some of their greatest opportunities in our desire to do what is right and good. They love to turn our strengths into points of weakness and vulnerability.

Several denominations, for example, have rightly discouraged the use of words that harm persons of various groups, gender exclusive words in speaking of God and words that stigmatize persons considered outside the normal range or outside the "in group" in various areas of society. This is one of the humane roles the Powers play in the ordering of society. No one is immune, however, to the distortion of which the Powers also are capable, and even the best intentions sometimes lead to questionable results.

The effort to change social views by the use of language is based, though many who engage in the effort are not aware of it, on a specific philosophical movement's view of the role language plays in our perception of reality. That school is *Postmodernism*. It teaches that there are no universal criteria or laws by which we can arrive at truth, declare good and evil, understand the past or interpret texts. The only reality, it teaches, is the reality we construct in our minds. We create the world by the language we use.

Postmodernism is onto something here. It correctly understands that words affect us, that words can help us or hurt us. Words affect a person's self-image. That is why Jesse Jackson's teaching school children to say "Black is beautiful" was so important.

As often happens with valid insights, however, the insight that language *usually affects perception* was transformed into the all-embracing assertion that language *inevitably effects reality*. The admonition to be sensitive in the use of words gave way to a prohibition of the use of certain words. Editorial boards and committees of newspapers, magazines, church publications, and television and radio corporations devised lists of words that are acceptable, words that are discouraged, and words that are prohibited. The Powers are out not only to help us, but to control us.

Actually, the manipulation of language does not always work. For several years, I worked with agencies that helped persons with various physical and mental difficulties. During those years, the words labeling the clients changed several times — from the *mentally handicapped* to *the mentally retarded* to *persons who are mentally retarded* to *persons with mental disabilities*, to *persons with developmental disabilities*. Since then, there have been other name changes, the purpose of each: to purify labels. Labels are necessary for purposes of aid and treatment, but labels carry their own dynamic. Shortly after the adoption of each new set of labels, those labels were associated with the clients and another set had to be adopted. Changing labels did not change the image. The new words soon took on the stereotypes associated with the persons.

Although many positive things can be said for the work of the Powers in political correctness, when valid insights about aspects of life become all-embracing ideologies, they thereby become idols. Political correctness is helpless to overcome attitudes born of the corruption of God's Creation. Pushed to extremes, it becomes a source of ridicule that undercuts the very goals it hopes to achieve, and the Powers, whose goal is confusion and alienation, win.

Questions for Discussion and Reflection:

1. What is your reaction to the assertion that nations and their institutions are embodiments of the Powers? Can you cite events from U.S. history that might reflect the positive role of the Powers? Can you cite events from U.S. history that might reflect the negative role of the Powers?

2. What are some implications of designating the Christian assembly (the church) a nation within nations? What are the implications of this for Christians being called into military service?

3. What elements of U.S. society today are enlightened by the author's account of the origins of the National Security Council and the Central Intelligence Agency? If you accept the author's perspective for a moment, in what ways might the Powers be seen to be at work in U.S. foreign and domestic policies today? What might be argued against that analysis?

4. What is you evaluation of or response to the author's theological analysis of the Holocaust? If you reject the author's analysis, what analysis would make in its place?

5. Why do you believe or not believe that the church and the synagogue (or Christians and Jews) are two branches of Israel, the People of God?

6. How do you usually define the word freedom? If we use Paul's definition of *freedom*, what is the difference between freedom and independence?

7. How does what you have considered justice compare with the author's definition of justice? On what basis would you challenge the author's definition?

8. What is your reaction to the author's description of true justice in the case of Medgar Evers and Byron De La Beckwith? Give reasons for your reaction.

9. How do you usually react to the term *political correctness*? Would you agree or disagree with the author's dual positive-negative analysis of political correctness? Give reasons for your answer.

10. Why do you agree or disagree with the author that our strengths can become our points of vulnerability? Give reasons for and examples of your answer.

Recognizing and Resisting the Powers

◈

Resistance, The Bible, And The Word Of God. Although the effects of the Powers are obvious, their nature is not obvious. Their existence and nature as Powers is revealed in Scripture. The Bible, therefore, is indispensable for the Christian assembly as the basic source for recognizing the Powers in their manifold appearances.

This does not mean an individualistic approach to the Bible. The Christian must study the Bible as a part of the Christian assembly across the centuries. The assembly in which the individual reads and reflects may be a congregation, a small group within a congregation, a gathering of individuals from several congregations, or individuals who for one reason or another are not affiliated with any congregation. Whatever its makeup, the assembly must read the Bible in the context of insights of Christians across the ages. In dialogue with these insights, the assembly reads the Bible in the context of the questions and conflicts of its own day, opening its mind to what God might speak in the present. The individual Christian may receive insights that the assembly can affirm. The assembly may receive insights that enlighten the individual. The individual may receive insights that the assembly rejects. The assembly may receive insights that the individual resists or rejects. It is even possible that we live in a time when God has abandoned the institutional church and that God will remain silent throughout our reading and reflecting. Some who sense the silence of God, but who are bothered by the word *abandoned*, say that God has handed the church over to the consequences of its own choices (in language similar to Romans 1), or that the situation of the church today is similar to that of the Judean Temple just before the Babylonian Exile. Both the Old and the New Testaments recognize the possibility that at times God's back may be turned on individuals, on groups, and even on the people of God (Amos 8:11–12; Psalm 22; Mark 15:34; Revelation 2:5; 3:16). In such a time, the assembly is to continue to read and reflect. When and if God does choose to speak to the assembly, the Bible may then be said to have become the Word of God to the assembly.

The Whole Armor Of God. Ephesians 6:11 does not urge us to take up weapons, but to put on armor from God. We are not to fight, but to engage in defensive wrestling. We are to be wary of the Powers and of their plots. In this, we do not depend upon our own craftiness or brilliance, but upon the power of God.

The one piece of armor in Ephesians 6:13–17 that might be used for offense is the sword — but even this is not the long sword of aggression, but the short sword for parrying the sword of the enemy. It is "the Spirit's sword — the word of God". It is not a sword to be used for of our own goals, but for the goals of the Spirit. Unfortunately, the church sometimes does attempt to wield the Spirit against whatever the church considers ungodly. All of us are susceptible to the illusion of having a corner on the truth and of being called to impose our views on the church, and on the entire society.

The sword of which Ephesians speaks is the Word of God. It comes *through* the Spirit, not to be used, but to be proclaimed. From the assembly's standpoint the Word is the proclamation that Jesus Christ seeks to liberate the world from the drives and forces that corrupt the life of the entire Creation. It is not an edict, but a news report. In the face of war, for example, it is not the command to turn the other cheek, but the news that God sets us free to offer the other cheek. In the face of capital punishment, it is not the argument that since Jesus wouldn't pull the switch or inject the serum, we should not do so, but the news that the cross liberates us to love and seek the rehabilitation of even the worst of criminals. The question is not "What would Jesus do?" but "How can we bear testimony of God's liberation?"

Resistance And The Assembly: The Spirit Vs. The Flesh. Resistance to the Powers is essentially the assembly's resistance. The individual participates in the assembly's resistance. The ability to resist comes from the Holy Spirit that God has poured out upon the assembly, bestowing upon the assembly both the *fruit of the Spirit* and *abilities of the Spirit*. The latter are the *charismata* (kaer-is-MA-tah), a plural Greek term usually translated *gifts of the Spirit.*

In Galatians 5:16–26, the Apostle Paul contrasts the *works of the flesh* with the *fruit of the Spirit*. The word *flesh* translates the Greek *sarx*, which on one level is the meaty substance of the body and on another level is the drive of self-interest, in whose bondage all of us live from birth. Paul usually uses *sarx* with the second meaning. The New Revised Standard Version's translation of the works of self-interest lists fornication, impurity, licentiousness, idolatry, sorcery, enmities, strife, jealousy, anger, quarrels, dissentions, factions, envy, drunkenness, carousing, and "things like these" (Galatians 5:19–21a). Much could be said of each word in this list, but it must suffice simply to point out two things.

1) The works of *sarx* are not vices or undesirable habits we can avoid by an act of the will. They are characteristics and actions produced by *sarx*. We do not choose them; they ensnare us. 2) The most important effect of *sarx* is the disruption of community.

The Spirit counteracts the works of *sarx* with the fruit of the Spirit. Despite the differences among the New Testament writers as to when the Spirit was poured out on the church (John 20:22–23; Acts 2:1–4) or whether it is Jesus, rather than the Holy Spirit, that will guide the church (Matthew 18:19–20; 28:18–20), for all three the result is the same: the Christian assembly is transformed and guided by one who represents God himself.

Just as two points were essential for understanding the works of sarx, two are essential for understanding the fruit of the Spirit. 1) The fruit of the Spirit is the character of the assembly produced by the Holy Spirit when the Spirit is not ignored or obstructed. 2) The fruit of the Spirit is not a set of virtues to be practiced for individual piety, but is attitudes and habits that nurture community. The presence of these characteristics reflects the inability of the Powers to gain control of the assembly.

Resistance And The Charismata: Abilities From The Spirit. In addition to transforming the assembly, the Spirit also equips the assembly by providing each individual with a charism (KA-rism) — an *ability* — the singular form of *charismata* — to enable the assembly to carry on its task. The lists of the *charismata* are not entirely alike from place to place (1 Corinthians 12:27–28; Romans 12:6–8; Ephesians 4:11–12), but their similarities are sufficient to indicate that Paul and his disciples had in mind specific functions essential for the assembly's ability to carry on its work.

The charismata are neither natural abilities with which individuals are born nor skills that can be learned or developed by attending school or participating in conferences or workshops. They are, quite simply, abilities given by the Spirit. Even if, for reasons known only to God, some individual's *charism* coincides with a "natural ability" or a skill, that is irrelevant from the standpoint of its identity as a *charism*.

The church sometimes has misunderstood this and has assumed that the church should turn to its own use the abilities and skills used by members of the congregation in their secular careers — for example, that church members who teach in the secular schools will make good church school teachers and that bankers, accountants, and stock market experts will make good church financial officials.

In both examples, the underlying assumption is that apart from their label as *religious* or *Christian*, church activities are no different from secular activities. In reality, the long-time use of secular school models for Christian education has resulted in disaster for most contemporary Christian education. Secular education theory assumes an unbiblical view of human nature and of the result of education. Secular education theory assumes the perfectibility of human beings through knowledge and group process and the perfectibility, or at least the improvement, of society through the improvement of individuals. In other words, secular education theory denies — implicitly, if not explicitly — that the Creation is fallen, that the present Age is dominated by the Powers, and that the transformation of human beings is solely the work of the Holy Spirit — not to mention that the death and resurrection of Jesus Christ is the decisive event in all history. Secular education, as beneficial, desirable and necessary as it is, is the work of the Powers.

Embodying the Powers, the banking systems of the world also operate on unbiblical assumptions and criteria. For example, medieval western society considered usury (charging money for the use of money) a sin, because it violates the Old Testament teaching that the People of God have a responsibility to care for those in need, and it undercuts the call of the Christian assembly to a life of unqualified love for others (*agape*). When money replaced the barter system as the basis of the world's economy, banks became basic institutions in the society, and in a fallen world banks cannot operate as charities. The necessity of banks as social institutions led the church to redefine usury as charging *excessive* interest. Today, banks, credit agencies, and all other institutions that engage in money exchange are guided by "what the traffic will bear." Many Christian groups, while campaigning against gambling, invest church funds in the stock market. In both, the object is to make money without labor — to let your money work for you. The Powers are at work in both.

When it is assumed that bankers automatically make good church treasurers or that stock brokers and accountants automatically make good members of the church finance committee, we see the ability of the Powers to blind even the people of God.

Resistance And Worship. The assembly resists the Powers through worship. Like the writer of Psalm 73, the assembly knows that the world is not the way that, apart from faith, it seems. In the world's eyes, the Powers — even if not called by that name by those who do not believe in them — are assumed to hold the upper hand. Evil and corruption, violence and hatred, power and influence have the last word. The Christian assembly, when faithful, knows better, and in worship it celebrates God's reassertion of sovereignty over the Creation and the basic defeat of the Powers in the death and resurrection of Jesus Christ.

True worship is focused on God. This is why biblical texts are crucial for liturgy. In the Psalms, for example, we hear the bold, precise affirmations of God's specific works in the life of Israel, in the Creation, and in the transcendent realm.

It is unfortunate that the church has so few hymns that celebrate the work of God in the history of the church. There are a few songs here and there, such as "Faith of our Fathers" (which, of course, can be easily reworded for purposes of inclusion without losing its testimony about those who faced peril, fire, and sword). Far too many of our hymns, however, are individualistic, self absorbed, and nostalgic. We could learn much from the liturgy of the synagogue, which, from start to finish, is a dialogue with God about God's role in Israel's history past and present.

Music appropriate to worship celebrates the sovereignty and character of God. Even good religious music that does not address God or affirm God's work, though it may be acceptable in other settings of the assembly, has no place in the service of worship. For example, music in which the congregation talks to itself or celebrates the emotions of the participants ("I Love to Tell the Story") has no place in worship. There is a world of difference between "O How I Love Jesus" and "Praise to the Lord, the Almighty, who rules all Creation!"

A good example of how hymns of thanksgiving can be distorted into pietistic songs of escapism is *Amazing Grace*. Written to celebrate God's deliverance of the writer from the Powers that produced the slave trade, *Amazing Grace* was transformed by the addition of a verse that turns away from a transformed life in this fallen world and concentrates on the infinite time of life in Heaven. It speaks of limitless time to sing God's praise when we finally get "there". The song no longer focuses on deliverance from the Powers in this world, but on the saving of the soul so the singer can "go to heaven."

In some churches today, the issue of proper forms for worship is more divisive than that of homosexuality. "Praise services" are to be found on every hand. New congregations spring up in order to engage in this kind of activity. Some congregations set aside an hour on Sunday or on Saturday evening for those who prefer a "praise service" to the "traditional service". In effect, the latter congregations have become two separate congregations sharing a common facility, and the seamless robe of Christ has again been torn asunder. Those who think that praise can only be done by snappy, repetitive music played on electric guitars and accompanied by drums are set against those who think that these can never be the means for true worship. Seeing the Body of Christ divided over the very thing that lies at the heart of the church's task — the worship of God — the Powers celebrate with glee.

The questions of music, prayers, creeds, responsive readings, and the like in true worship are correctly answered with a few simple observations: (1) In genuine worship the Christian assembly celebrates the sovereign rule of the God of Jesus Christ over the nations, institutions, and systems of the world, over human history, and over the entire Creation. (2) Whatever contributes to that celebration has a place in worship. (3) Anything that either detracts from that celebration or does not contribute to it has no place in worship. (4) Evaluation of worship on the basis of these criteria is properly a matter of assembly consensus, not of either democratic vote or individual declaration.

The true worship of God will not be nationalistic, but will affirm the absolute sovereignty of the God of Abraham and Sarah, of Isaac and Rebecca, of Jacob and Rachel and Leah, and of Jesus Christ over all nations. All nationally conscious worship or worship that celebrates elements of the national culture is worship of the Power of the nation and, as such, pays homage not to God, but to the Powers.

A form of worship once important in the life of the church, but now found mostly in monastic orders, is the observance of the divine hours. At set times each day, the community gathers to praise God by prayers, the chanting of psalms and other acts of worship. The form also has survived in congregations that observe morning and evening prayer each day and is now being practiced here and there by individuals and small groups using resources beginning to appear from several publishers.

When properly observed, the Hours are not instances of isolated individuals engaging in moments of piety, but are occasions when the People of God, even if scattered as groups and individual persons, pause to celebrate the sovereignty of God over the Creation. Set hours assure that throughout the day and night, gatherings of the People of God are together engaged in one element of their vocation — the praise of God.

In the final analysis, our call is to gather and worship. Our efforts become true worship, however, only when the Holy Spirit or the faithful angels take our efforts and blend them with the worship of the heavenly choirs. That is why we commonly hear the plea " accept our prayer" or "accept our worship."

Resistance And Prayer. Prayer is both a major means of resistance to the Powers and the place at which the Powers make one of their strongest attacks. Even some Christians regard prayer as pointless and sometimes dismiss it as autosuggestion. God, it is said, is neither egotistical nor fickle and does not change plans on the basis of uninformed human desires. Nevertheless, regardless of what God may be in and of God's self, God's interaction with the world is experienced in ways that from the human standpoint can only be described as God condescending to human interventions.

As resistance, prayer is a community work. It is a recognition that our lives and the life of the entire Creation are in the hands of God. It is the confession that God is sovereign. Even when prayer is struggle with God, as in Jesus' effort to persuade God of a specific course of action, it is a struggle of one subjected to God, regardless of God's response or lack of response. Prayer accompanies God's gift of the armor of resistance.

We can and do pray for all sorts of reasons, but the only unassailable reason for praying is obedience. Prayer must be commanded because true prayer is neither easy nor natural. The pretenders (the *hypocrites* — those who hide behind a mask) described in the Sermon on the Mount (Matthew 6:5) consider prayer to be easy. They make a show of their prayer in order to earn a reputation for themselves. They pray in all sorts of public places, at all sorts of public meetings. It is not clear to which god they pray, especially in secular gatherings such as political rallies, civic clubs, sports events, national and state prayer breakfasts, and governmental inaugurations, since secular gatherings are not under the patronage of the God of Israel and of Jesus Christ, but of the angels assigned to the nations, the Powers, or — since all these fall under the Old Age — perhaps of Satan himself. In this context, it is not frivolous to say that if you really wish to see Devil worship, attend some of the events named above.

Of course, the people involved will not say they are worshipping the Devil, but the god they worship will be the god who blesses this nation and fights for the nation against other nations — the god that says, "defeat the enemy," the god that says, "If you aid and abet the enemy you are guilty of treason." To truly pray as a Christian assembly is to commit treason against the nation in which the assembly resides, regardless of the nation. But those who pray to the national gods — to the Powers — offer what they seem to consider genuine prayer. It is all so easy.

The Apostle Paul tells us that prayer is not easy. Part of our weakness is that we do not even know how to pray *as we ought* (Romans 8:26). If we take Paul seriously, prayer as it should be prayed not only is not easy; for human beings — even Christians — it is impossible. All sorts of things frustrate and distract us — time, worry, fear, doubt, self-interest, anticipated pleasures, other duties — as the Powers seek to divert and defeat us. There should be no wonder that the Roman Catholic tradition long ago decided that we need saints to intercede for us.

How then are we to obey the command to pray? How are we to accept Jesus' invitation to pray the Lord's Prayer? Is this not an example of what some have called "Paul's distortion of the simple teachings of Jesus?" Not at all. We address God not under the illusion that it is within our power to reach God, but with the assurance that we have an advocate who intercedes for us with sighs too deep for any human words — the Holy Spirit (Romans 8:27). Our time and space bound efforts at prayer become true prayer when, and only when, the Holy Spirit takes them and makes of them transcendent intercessions beyond our power to imagine.

A major obstruction to our efforts at prayer is the character of the time in which we live — a time so desolate that, as already mentioned, some suspect that God has abandoned the institutional church. There are things that suggest validity to that suspicion — the commercialization of the church by hawking its services as just another product to give personal satisfaction in the face of the daily routine; the politicization of the church by making it the advocate of secular national goals; the abandonment of the church's identity as holy nation by adopting the values of the secular world as criteria for ministry; consumer testing to see what will attract people to the church's activities, including worship, thus determining the church's life by the works of sarx, not by the fruit of the Spirit and the charismata.

If in fact God has abandoned the institutional church, it is safe to say that God did not initiate the abandonment; the church did. Further, in such a time, is prayer not irrelevant or perhaps even blasphemous? On the contrary, it is precisely in such a time that prayer becomes most urgent — the prayer that God will have mercy upon the church, liberate it from the bonds of Sin, and use it as a redeeming force in the world — a Prayer of opposition against the Powers.

Questions for Discussion or Reflection:

1. Using two or three different translations, read Ephesians 6:14–17 aloud in the group. Spend some time reflecting on the meaning of each item in the list. Note that words normally used in military defense are defined in terms of elements of the life of faith. What thoughts come to mind on each of the items?

2. Do you participate in a group that regularly reads the Bible together? If so, tell of some experiences of the group. If not, would you like to do so? How might you go about finding or forming such group?

3. Christians frequently argue over whether the Bible IS the Word of God or CONTAINS the word of God. How do you interpret each of these? Compare these with the concept in the book that the Bible BECOMES the Word of God.

4. Give your reactions to the authors descriptions for each of the following terms: sarx, the fruit of the Spirit, the abilities of the Spirit. How does the author's interpretation of *the flesh* compare with your previous understanding of the word?

5. Using two or three translations of the Bible, read aloud Galatians 5:19–24. Spend some time discussing each term in the passage and comparing the translations of those terms.

6. Does your congregation or group consider anything similar to the *charismata* when developing tasks for the members? Why or why not? Do you know people who you think have abilities from the Spirit that are not used? In what practical ways might a group or congregation go about determining the *charismata* of its members?

7. Do you agree or disagree with the author's description of the presuppositions (or assumptions) of secular education? Explain your answer.

8. What does the assertion that in worship the world's true condition is celebrated mean to you? Do you usually think of worship in these terms? Why or why not?

9. Are you part of a congregation or group that feels the effects of the debate over praise services? What is your reaction to the author's observations about the different approaches to worship? If you are part of a group that is facing this issue, what constructive steps have been taken to deal with the issue?

10. Describe and evaluate the worship in which you participate.

11. Why do you agree or disagree with the author about what music is acceptable for worship?

12. Read Romans 8:26–27 aloud. What is your reaction to Paul's analysis? What is your reaction to the book's description of the ways the Powers interfere with prayer?

13. What is your reaction to the suggestion that God may have, for the moment, abandoned the institutional church? Why is this your reaction? Would you agree with one of the other descriptions of the plight of the institutional church? Why or why not?

14. What is your evaluation of the book as a whole? Has it caused you to change your mind in any way? Has it confirmed you in some of your prior beliefs? Has it done neither? If it has none neither, why do think this is the case?

Suggestions for Further Study

Ellul, Jacques. *Hope in Time of Abandonment*, *The New Demons*, and *Prayer and Modern Man* (All three of these books are out of print, but are available from out-of-print sources on the Internet and are well worth finding.)

Ellul, Jacques. *The Presence of the Kingdom*. (Helmers and Howard Publishers, 1989.)

Lewis, C.S. *That Hideous Strength* (Scribner, 1996)

O'Connor, Flannery. *Complete Stories* (Noonday Press, 1996)

Stringfellow, William. *An Ethic for Christians and Other Aliens in a Strange Land* (Out of print, but available from out-of-print sources on the Internet. Well worth finding.)

Tickle, Phyllis. *The Divine Hours* (3 volumes, Doubleday)

Wink, Walter. *The Powers That Be: Theology for a New Millennium* (Galilee, 1999)

Other books from the Insights series include:

www.ingramcontent.com/pod-product-compliance
Lightning Source LLC
LaVergne TN
LVHW051712080426
835511LV00017B/2864